Contents

Introduction.....
Mute Swan......
Whooper Swan..
Greylag Goose..
Shelduck.......
Wigeon........
Teal............
Mallard...................17
Tufted Duck............19
Eider...................21
Red-breasted Merganser.23
Red Grouse.............25
Red-throated Diver......27
Fulmar.................29
Storm Petrel............31
Gannet.................33
Cormorant.............35
Shag...................37
Grey Heron.............39
Moorhen...............41
Oystercatcher...........43
Golden Plover..........45
Lapwing................47
Ringed Plover..........49
Whimbrel..............51
Curlew.................53
Turnstone..............55
Sanderling.............57
Dunlin.................59
Red-necked Phalarope...61
Common Sandpiper.....63
Redshank..............65
Snipe..................67
Arctic Skua............69
Great Skua.............71
Puffin.................73
Black Guillemot........75
Razorbill................77

Herring Gull.............93
Great Black-backed Gull..95
Rock Dove.............97
Wood Pigeon...........99
Collared Dove..........101
Merlin.................103
Rook..................105
Hooded Crow..........107
Raven.................109
Goldcrest..............111
Skylark................113
Swallow...............115
Chiffchaff..............117
Willow Warbler.........119
Blackcap..............121
Wren..................123
Starling...............125
Blackbird..............127
Robin.................129
Wheatear..............131
House Sparrow........133
Grey Wagtail..........135
White Wagtail.........137
Meadow Pipit.........139
Rock Pipit.............141
Chaffinch..............143
Linnet.................145
Twite.................147
Common Redpoll.......149
Siskin.................151

Introduction

This small guide is intended for visitors to Shetland who wish to identify the birds they see while they are in the islands. It focuses on the summer months so includes those species that breed in Shetland along with a few others that are regular summer visitors but do not breed here.

Photographs should help to identify the species. Where the sexes differ in plumage a second inset photograph is provided.

The approximate length of each species gives you an idea of their size. Length is shown at 1/20 scale.

Length: 100cm

◀─────────────────────────▶

Brief details of the habitat you are most likely to see each species in is also provided. Each page is colour coded to give an indication of the habitat the colours and broad habitats are as follows:

Lochs/burns
Sea/coasts/cliffs
Moorlands/grasslands
Gardens/plantations

The breeding status is given based on the number of breeding pairs present in the islands. This will give you an indication as to how likely it is to see the species concerned.

●	●	●	●	Abundant	over 1,000 breeding pairs
●	●	●	○	Common	100-1,000 breeding pairs
●	●	○	○	Scarce	10-99 breeding pairs
●	○	○	○	Rare	fewer than 10 breeding pairs
○	○	○	○	Does not breed	

Finally, some Shetland names are provided for interest. They appear in top right where relevant.

Mute Swan

Length: 150cm

Breeding Status: Rare

● ○ ○ ○

Habitat: Large nutrient rich freshwater lochs

The Mute Swan is easily told from its cousin the Whooper Swan by its orange not yellow bill. It also has a more graceful appearance, with more curvature in the neck, and a more pointed tail. Males can be told from females by the larger, more swollen black knob at the base of the bill.

Attempts to introduce Mute Swans to Shetland in the early 1900s failed but the species colonised naturally in the 1990s, although many breeding attempts are unsuccessful. Despite their name Mute Swans can be quite noisy during courtship, uttering various snorting and grunting noises. Females will often carry their cygnets on their back during the first few days after hatching.

Whooper Swan

Length: 150cm

<--->

Breeding Status: Rare

● ○ ○ ○

Habitat: Large nutrient rich freshwater lochs and adjacent grassland

Whooper Swans first bred in Shetland in 1994 and there are now about ten pairs in the islands. They seem to enjoy greater breeding success here than their close cousin the Mute Swan even though it is typical that a high proportion of adult Whoopers do not breed some years. Shetland's breeders originated from Iceland.

As with many wildfowl, pairs will often remain together for life. The female incubates the eggs while the male remains close by ready to defend the nest from intruders. At this time males can be so aggressive that they will attack anything large and white – even sheep. Both adults care for the cygnets. Swans generally do not breed until they are four or five years old and can expect to live 10-20 years.

Greylag Goose

Length: 80cm

←——————————————→

Breeding Status: Common

● ● ● ○

Habitat: Moorland, grassland and large freshwater lochs

The Greylag is the only species of goose likely to be seen in Shetland during the summer. They only started breeding here in the mid-1980s but the population has now numbers over 1,000 pairs! Small flocks of non-breeding birds also occur and any hill walk in Shetland is likely to be accompanied by the honking of Greylag Geese.

Inadvertently we have created ideal conditions for Greylag Geese in Shetland. Their favoured moorland breeding haunts and the large freshwater lochs which offer safety for the growing goslings, and moulting, flightless adults, has always been here but agricultural improvement of grassland has now provided them with an ideal food source too. This has encouraged many birds to remain here to breed, rather than risk migrating back to Iceland for the summer.

Shelduck

Length: 60cm

<————————————————>

Breeding Status: Rare

● ○ ○ ○

Habitat: Sheltered coastline and freshwater lochs

The Shelduck is restricted to the South Mainland of Shetland as a breeding species where they nest in burrows. Typically males outnumber females in Shetland in spring and this may be a result of females being predated by introduced ground predators while they are incubating. Notice how the bill base is more swollen in the male of this pair than the female.

Both adults remain with the ducklings after they hatch and this helps to fend off potential predators notably Great Skuas and gulls. Despite this most broods are soon lost, some within just 24 hours of hatching. One notable pair at Boddam deserve great credit, managing to raise all their ducklings every year!

Wigeon

Length: 46cm

<------------------>

Breeding Status: Rare

● ○ ○ ○

Habitat: Freshwater lochs with emergent vegetation and adjacent short grassland

The male is distinctive but the female is more subtle. She shows some warm rufous tones, has a relatively large, rounded head, and a small blue-grey bill. Wigeon favour lochs with emergent vegetation in which they can hide their ducklings, although adults are often seen grazing on short grassland adjacent to lochs.

The males are usually more obvious than the females during the breeding season. As with many wildfowl they take no part in rearing the ducklings. Instead they leave the female to hatch the eggs and swap their showy breeding plumage for a more cryptic 'eclipse' plumage that blends in better with their surroundings while they moult their feathers.

Teal

Length: 36cm

←――――――→

Breeding Status: Common

● ● ● ○

Habitat: Freshwater lochs and pools

As with other dabbling ducks the male is distinctive but the female is more difficult to identify. Although superficially similar to a Mallard they are only half its size and tend to forage more inconspicuously in emergent vegetation in the shallows. They can take off almost vertically and are fast and agile in flight, often forming tight flocks.

The term dabbling relates to they way these ducks 'up-end' when they are searching for invertebrates, seeds or other plant matter. Like all wildfowl the female only starts incubation when her last egg is laid. This ensures that all the ducklings are born at the same time and can quickly be led away from the nest to find shelter and food. The ducklings feed themselves but mum continues to brood them for a few days.

Mallard

Length: 55cm

<----------------------------->

Breeding Status: Common

● ● ● ○

Habitat: Freshwater lochs, pools and larger burns

This is the commonest dabbling duck in Shetland and the ancestor of many varieties of domestic duck. Although males are distinctive, females are similar to other dabbling ducks. They are larger and more bulky, with a longish bill and rounded head. They have a dark eyestripe and pale supercilium, and usually show some orange on the bill.

Females nest in dense vegetation, sometimes a fair distance from the nearest water. Clutches are large and can equate to more than 70% of the female's body weight. The largest number of eggs found in one nest in Shetland is 17, although these could have been laid by more than one female. Once hatched, mum quickly marches the ducklings down to the relative safety of the nearest water body.

Tufted Duck

Length: 44cm

Breeding Status: Scarce

●●○○

Habitat: Freshwater lochs

The Tufted Duck is the most common diving duck in Shetland. Unlike the dabbling ducks that 'up-end' for their food, diving ducks dive under the water for theirs, meaning they can inhabit deeper lochs. The males are distinctive with their black and white plumage and obvious crest but females are a little more difficult to identify. They also show crests, or some raised feathering at the rear of the crown, but are a fairly uniform brown, with slightly paler flanks and occasionally some whitish around the base of the bill.

The breeding population in Shetland has increased in recent years and pairs can now be found on most of the larger islands. They are always present at the Loch of Spiggie in South Mainland.

Eider

Length: 65cm

←——————————→

Breeding Status: Abundant

● ● ● ●

Habitat: Coasts

The Eider is our most common sea duck and is rarely seen on fresh water. Males are distinctive but females are a uniform neatly dark-barred brown. Young males, initially blackish with a pale breast and spot on the rear flanks, show more white as they get older.

The cryptic female rarely leaves the nest once her eggs are laid, spending 99% of her time incubating. She can lose up to 40% of her body weight during this period! Females often bring their broods together to form large crèches. As well as reducing the risk of predation this enables females to take it in turns to replenish themselves with some much needed food. The insulating properties of Eider down are, of course, legendary.

Red-breasted Merganser

Length: 55cm

←——————————————→

Breeding Status: Scarce

● ● ○ ○

Habitat: Large freshwater lochs and sheltered coasts

The long, slender bill of this species is very distinctive compared to our other breeding ducks. The inner edge of the bill is finely serrated allowing it to grasp fish. Groups can sometimes be seen fishing together, moving rapidly inshore, forcing fish into shallow water where they are easier to catch.

The males gaudy plumage serves it well during courtship but is replaced early in the summer once it has mated. As with all wildfowl the resulting plumage, known as 'eclipse' plumage, is very similar to that of the female. The longish, slim body becomes greyish contrasting with the brownish head and neck. This enables the male to blend in much better with its surroundings during the period when it moults and becomes flightless.

Red Grouse

Length: 36cm

<—————>

Breeding Status: Common

● ● ● ○

Habitat: Moorlands

The Red Grouse is the only grouse found in Shetland. It was introduced to the islands from mainland Britain although it is unclear when. We know this as Shetland birds remain brown in winter like their Scottish counterparts, whereas continental birds moult into a white winter plumage. Red Grouse can be found on Mainland, Bressay and Whalsay.

The bulk of the grouse's diet comprises heather, although cotton-grass and the fruiting capsules of mosses are favoured when available as they contain more essential nutrients. Chicks leave the nest when they are a day old and prefer invertebrates as they contain the protein necessary for growth. Like the adults, chicks have feathers all the way down to their toes.

Red-throated Diver

Length: 61cm

←――――――――→

Breeding Status: Common

● ● ● ○

Habitat: Freshwater lochs, flying to the sea to feed

The species has a very distinctive shape with its flat forehead and slim bill, often held above the horizontal. Its grey head and neck and maroon throat are also distinctive, although the throat can look blackish at distance. It will breed on even the smallest hill lochs providing there is enough space to allow take off.

Shetland holds about 30% of the British breeding population. The species is afforded special protection making it an offence to disturb it near the nest. The wailing, cackling and cooing calls of a courting or territorial pair, demands attention. Local folklore suggests that divers can forecast the weather: "when the rain goose makes for the sea take up your boats and head for the lee, when the rain goose makes for the hill set down your boats and make where you will."

Fulmar

Length: 48cm

◄──────────►

Breeding Status: Abundant

● ● ● ●

Habitat: Cliffs, inland rock faces and quarries

The Fulmar is often confused with gulls but note the long, straight wings and stiff-winged flight, and when ashore, how it sits on its haunches rather than standing on its legs. Look carefully and you will see the tube-like nostrils situated on top of the bill, just like other petrels and its close relatives the albatrosses. Every individual has a unique colour pattern on these nostrils.

The Fulmar is now our most common seabird numbering over 200,000 pairs, yet it didn't breed in the islands until 1878. The provision of food – offal and discards from a burgeoning fishing industry – undoubtedly fed this increase. The Fulmar is one of our longest-lived birds, some reaching the grand old age of 50. Keep your distance mind, the adults and chicks can both spit a foul-smelling oil that lingers on clothing!

Storm Petrel

Length: 15cm
←→

Breeding Status: Abundant
● ● ● ●

Habitat: Only on offshore islands and at sea

The Storm Petrel remains well offshore during the day where it picks its food from the sea surface and converts it into an energy rich oil to feed to its chicks. The tiny tube nose is thought to be linked to a heightened sense of smell enabling it to locate food when out at sea. Adults only come back to the colonies under cover of darkness to avoid would-be predators such as Bonxies and gulls.

Incubation and chick-rearing shifts may last several days while the other adult is away feeding; chicks can even reduce their body temperature and enter a state of torpor if food is in short supply. The best way to see the species is to take one of the special evening trips to Mousa, when the birds can be heard singing in the dykes and seen flying around the 2,000 year old broch.

Gannet

Length: 91cm

Breeding Status: Abundant

● ● ● ●

Habitat: Cliffs

The Gannet is our largest, and currently most successful, seabird. Its long wingspan enables it to forage efficiently over large distances and it can feed on sandeels, large shoaling fish like mackerel and on discards from fishing boats. Young birds are brown and gradually acquire there black and white adult plumage over 4 or 5 years.

Although there are only four breeding colonies in Shetland, Gannets are commonly seen offshore. If you are lucky you might even witness them diving arrow-like, wings swept back head outstretched, into the sea after shoaling fish. They hit the water at great speed and have air sacs in their face and chest which protect them from the impact. Young Gannets can be so well fed that when they fledge all they can do is glide down to the sea where they sit, losing weight for a few days, until they can fly.

Cormorant

Length: 85cm

Breeding Status: Common

● ● ● ○

Habitat: Offshore stacks, occasionally visiting fresh water

Cormorants and Shags are easily confused even though Cormorants look markedly larger when the two are seen together. The Shag is by far the more common species in Shetland occurring along much of our coastline but avoids fresh water. Cormorants breed on just a few offshore stacks but feeding birds can be seen in the sheltered sounds between the islands, and are much more likely on fresh water where they will take impossibly large trout.

Adult Cormorants have a purple-blue sheen to their plumage and extensive yellow facial skin with a white patch encircling it, and a white thigh patch. The yellow is restricted to the gape in shags and their plumage is uniform with an oily-green sheen. Cormorants often fly high above the water, in contrast, Shags tend to hug the sea.

Shag

Length: 73cm

←——————————————→

Breeding Status: Abundant

● ● ● ●

Habitat: Cliffs and boulder beaches

Shags and Cormorants often stand in groups on coastal rocks or headland with their wings held out. The function of this is unclear; could it be to dry the wings, aid digestion, or even be a form of communication? Immatures are often present. They are browner and less glossy than adults, with pale necks and brownish bellies. The pattern is reversed in young Cormorants which show darker necks and whitish bellies.

Shags build bulky nests on cliffs or boulder beaches. Their rather prehistoric looking young are born blind and featherless. Incubation commences as soon as the first egg is laid so the young hatch sequentially. If food is plentiful then all four or five of the brood may fledge but if food is scarce the oldest chick will demand the food. This strategy may ensure that at least one or two chicks survive even when fish are in short supply.

Grey Heron

Length: 93cm

<----------------------------->

Breeding Status: Scarce non-breeding summer visitor

O O O O

Habitat: Sheltered coats and freshwater locks

The Grey Heron bred in Shetland a handful of times some years ago. Herons are typically colonial and nest in trees, the breeding attempts in Shetland were of single pairs on the cliffs! A few non-breeding individuals occur every summer, however, usually found along sheltered voes or at larger freshwater lochs with well-vegetated edges where they will sometimes defend feeding territories.

In flight the Heron has slow, deep wingbeats on bowed wings, with the head and neck drawn in. When fishing, they remain motionless, or walk slowly with their neck muscles tensed, ready to grasp or stab their prey. Eels seem to be a popular prey item in Shetland.

Moorhen

Length: 29cm

←————→

Breeding Status: Scarce

● ● ○ ○

Habitat: Freshwater lochs with vegetated edges

Moorhens are usually seen walking around the damp edges of lochs or swimming along with a typical jerking head action. The red frontal shield is obvious in both sexes and is probably important in courtship and territorial defence. Previously restricted to the South Mainland as a breeding species, pairs are now appearing further afield where there is suitable habitat as the population increases.

Both sexes share incubation and chick-rearing and the young leave the nest soon after hatching. They look quite comical – balls of dark down with a bald forehead, thick legs and huge long toes that look disproportionately large, but are very useful for spreading the birds weight when walking on vegetation floating on the loch surface.

Oystercatcher

Length: 42cm

<———————>

Breeding Status: Abundant

● ● ● ●

Habitat: Coastlines, moorland and grassland

An unmistakable wader, with its pied plumage and long, bright orange bill. Arguably Shetland's most common wader and certainly our noisiest one! The rather monotonous 'cleeping' sound is an almost constant companion when outside walking during the early summer. If the chicks are approached too closely then the aggrieved parent becomes almost hysterical, circling the intruder and uttering a constant piping sound.

The Oystercatcher is unique among British waders. They often pair for life which is unusual for a wader, but even more remarkably, they provide food for their chicks up to and sometimes beyond fledging. Despite their name, however, they do not eat oysters; earthworms, insect larvae and shellfish are the main prey.

Golden Plover

Length: 26cm

Breeding Status: Abundant

● ● ● ●

Habitat: Moorland

The only medium sized wader likely to be encountered with spangled golden plumage, an open face and a short bill. The black belly is shared only with the much smaller Dunlin among Shetland's breeding waders. The piping whistle and aerial song flight are among the most evocative sounds ringing out from its moorland breeding habitat.

The female plover lays her eggs over a period of several days but does not start to incubate these until the last has been laid, ensuring that all the chicks hatch at about the same time. The chicks also start calling a few days before hatching and this too helps synchronise hatching. As with all waders, the parent is quick to move the chicks away from the nest to safety once they hatch.

Lapwing

Length: 30cm

<——————>

Breeding Status: Abundant

● ● ● ●

Habitat: Damp grassland and moorland

The black and white plumage, crest and rounded wings are distinctive but in good light the dark upperparts come to life with beautiful iridescent shades of green and purple. Add to this the noise of the beating wings during its acrobatic courtship display flight, and its hoarse 'pee-wit' call and this is one very special wader. Breeding adults will follow intruders for some distance to ensure that their eggs or chicks are safe. Look carefully from the confines of a vehicle and the chicks will often reveal themselves.

The species has declined markedly on mainland Britain following agricultural intensification but the Shetland population is faring better. Lapwings can replace their clutches up to four times if they are lost; each laid five to 12 days after the previous one.

Ringed Plover

Length: 18cm

Breeding Status: Common

● ● ● ○

Habitat: Beaches, short coastal turf and bare areas inland

This is the only small plover with a black and white head pattern, white collar and black breast band likely to be seen in the islands. Despite this rather striking appearance, however, the adult just melts away into a gravel track, or pebble beach once it sits on its nest. The eggs and chicks too, are wonderfully camouflaged so take great care where you walk if you see an agitated Ringed Plover on the beach.

This is one of the first waders to lay its eggs in spring. They share a lovely, slow butterfly-like display flight with the Golden Plover and Oystercatcher. Ringed Plovers are also masters at feigning injury; get too close to the nest and they will hold their wings as if broken, looking like an easy meal for a predator. They are quick to find a miracle cure though, flying off once they have drawn the intruder away from the nest.

Whimbrel

Length: 41cm

←――――→

Breeding Status: Common

● ● ● ○

Habitat: Moorlands

The Whimbrel is smaller than the Curlew, with a shorter bill that is decurved more towards its tip and a more striking head pattern comprising a series of dark and pale stripes over the head. Its call – a loud rapid whistling 'tu-tu-tu-tu-tu-tu' is also quite different from the Curlew's more mournful 'cur-loo'.

Shetland hosts around 95% of Britain's breeding Whimbrel but the population has been declining here although it is unclear why. It nests on blanket bogs and on the serpentine heath of Unst and Fetlar, where it likes to nest on tussocks from which it can view its surroundings. The chicks are often taken to insect-rich wet runnels or reseeds to feed.

Curlew

Length: 53cm

Breeding Status: Abundant

● ● ● ●

Habitat: Rough grassland and moorland

The Curlew can only really be mistaken with the Whimbrel but is larger, has a longer, more evenly decurved bill and a less striking head pattern, although the supercilium and eyestripe can be surprisingly well-marked. The Curlew's bubbling song, given as it displays around its breeding territory, is the equivalent of a dawn chorus for many Shetlanders.

The Curlew has declined markedly on mainland Britain and is now listed on the Red List of Birds of Conservation Concern. Here in Shetland, however, where the climate is severe and the soils relatively poor, agricultural intensification has not occurred to the same degree, and as a result the Curlew population is showing no signs of a decrease.

Turnstone

Length: 22cm
←——→

Breeding Status: Common non-breeding summer visitor
O O O O

Habitat: Beaches, shallow rocky coastlines and short grassland

The pied plumage, short orange legs and short, slightly wedge-shaped bill, make this small to medium-sized wader rather distinctive. The photograph shows a spanking adult in summer plumage; non-breeding birds show a similar plumage pattern but are duller and lack the bright chestnut tones.

The species has never bred in Shetland which is perhaps surprising as it breeds at similar latitudes in Scandinavia and in habitat not dissimilar to that found in Shetland. So, keep your eyes open – you might find the first British breeding pair! As the name suggests they turn over stones to search for food, but will also use their bills to dig and probe, and even as a hammer to crack open shells.

Sanderling

Length: 19cm
←——→

Breeding Status: Scarce non-breeding summer visitor
○ ○ ○ ○

Habitat: Sandy beaches

The Sanderling is a smallish wader, similar in size to the much more common Dunlin, but with a shorter, straight bill. In summer plumage it is quite different with chestnut tones to its upperparts, reddish tones to its face, throat and neck, and white underparts. Its feeding behaviour can be distinctive too, dashing along the tideline like high-speed clockwork toys, one moment scampering before an advancing wave, then instantly turning to follow it back out again to search for food.

Sanderlings breed in the high Arctic. Some are still migrating north through Shetland in June, while failed breeders are already heading south again in mid to late July! Some perform astonishingly lengthy migrations, with a return trip between their breeding and wintering grounds in excess of 30,000 kilometres!

Dunlin

Length: 19cm

←—→

Breeding Status: Abundant

● ● ● ●

Habitat: Moorlands, sometimes feeding along the coast

The most commonly encountered small wader in Shetland at any season. It has a dumpy appearance, relatively short legs and a slightly decurved bill, the length of which varies between individuals. It is a lot easier to identify in summer when it has a black belly and brighter, chestnut upperparts. When breeding it favours high quality, wet blanket bogs but will often visit freshwater pools and the coast to feed.

Like many waders that breed at high latitude and winter in more temperate southern climes, the summer plumage is much more upmarket than that in winter. The bright, often striking, summer plumage blends in well with tundra or moorland breeding habitat, while the dull grey winter plumage blends in better with the muddy estuaries where the birds spend their winter.

Red-necked Phalarope

Length: 18cm

←——→

Breeding Status: Scarce

● ● ○ ○

Habitat: Wet pools with emergent vegetation

A very distinctive small wader best looked for at the Loch of Funzie on Fetlar, where it can sometimes be seen swimming in the shallows picking freshly emerged insects from stones and emergent vegetation. Shetland is THE premier place in Britain to see this stunning, confiding wader.

Phalaropes have an unusual breeding biology. The females are brighter than the males and once they have mated lay their clutch of eggs leaving him to incubate them and raise the chicks. Then they search for another male, establish a brief pair bond with him, and lay a further clutch of eggs for him to incubate. Recent research undertaken in Shetland has shown that our breeding phalaropes winter in the Galapagos!

Common Sandpiper

Length: 19cm

←——→

Breeding Status: Scarce

● ● ○ ○

Habitat: Freshwater lochs and burns

This small to medium-sized wader is best identified by its distinctive behaviour and shape. It is best looked for in North and West Mainland, where it can be found frenetically bobbing up and down, pumping its tail, along burn sides or on the stony shores of freshwater lochs. It adopts a very horizontal position, often appearing to crouch, and has a relatively short neck, legs and bill but a long tail. Its flight is also distinctive being stiff-winged and comprising shallow, almost flicking wingbeats, interspersed with short glides.

If you find an adult then look carefully and you might see the chicks as well. In common with all waders their legs and feet seem disproportionately large – they have to be, as most wader chicks have to feed themselves as soon as they hatch.

63

Redshank

Length: 25cm
←——→

Breeding Status: Abundant
● ● ● ●

Habitat: Wet areas on grassland and moorland

The Redshank is easily identified courtesy of its long red legs. Its loud whistling call note 'teuw-who-who' is also diagnostic and a common sound of the foreshore. In flight, look for a white back and trailing edge to the inner wing. Redshanks favour damp areas with enough cover to provide shelter and food for their chicks and will often nest near to Lapwings, taking advantage of that species' aggressive nature.

Although typically quiet and wary during incubation they soon turn the volume up when the chicks hatch, often flying above an intruder, uttering a constant high pitched alarm call. As well as trying to force the intruder to leave, the parent is signalling to its chick to stay still; it is much easier for a predator to see a moving chick than one hiding in long vegetation.

Snipe

Length: 25cm

◄───────►

Breeding Status: Abundant

● ● ● ●

Habitat: Wet areas in rough grassland and moorlands

The Snipe's cryptic plumage, grating calls and distinctive zig-zag escape flight when flushed at close quarters, are distinctive. The chicks, if seen, are equally cryptic with wonderful burnt orange or purplish tones admixed with buff and ashy grey. The stunning display flight, when the males dive almost vertically downwards forcing air to pass through the outer tail feather to produce a drumming noise, is typical of a warm summer evening.

Once hatched waders split their chicks up, so that if a predator finds one it will not automatically find the others. In Snipe the male will often care for the first one or two chicks to hatch, leaving the female to care for the remainder; the pair may not see each other again.

Arctic Skua

Length: 41cm

←—————→

Breeding Status: Scarce

● ● ○ ○

Habitat: Moorlands but feeds at sea

Much smaller and slimmer than the Great Skua, with long, pointed central tail feathers. It is also considerably more agile than its larger cousin. Arctic Skuas come in two colour phases – light and dark, with the dark form vastly outnumbering pale ones here in Shetland. Unfortunately the population has declined markedly in recent years as a result of a shortage of sandeels and predation by Great Skuas.

The Arctic Skua is a kleptoparasite: it chases other birds, notably Kittiwakes, Arctic Terns and Puffins, forcing them to disgorge their food. Both the Arctic and Great Skua can be pretty uncompromising if you walk close to their nests but while Great Skuas generally 'attack' from the front and rarely make contact, Arctic Skuas come from behind and will frequently clip the back of the intruders neck with their feet!

Great Skua

Length: 54cm

<——————————————————>

Breeding Status: Abundant

● ● ● ●

Habitat: Moorlands but feeds at sea

Only really confusable with immature gulls but the plumage is all dark mottled brown, while in flight the large white wing patches are diagnostic. In a global context the Great Skua is Shetland's most important seabird with around 40% of the world population breeding here. Yet because of its predatory habits it does not enjoy a good reputation in the islands.

Following the sandeel crash in the 1980s and the tightening up of regulations on discarding fish from fishing vessels more recently, the Great Skua has been forced to seek alternative food. Seabirds have fulfilled this need and Arctic Skuas, Kittiwakes and Puffins in particular have been targeted. Skuas have even begun to kill adult Gannets in recent years!

Puffin

Length: 31cm

←——————→

Breeding Status: Abundant

● ● ● ●

Habitat: Cliffs

Although Puffins have quite a widespread distribution in the islands, the population has declined in recent years. Sumburgh Head is the most accessible reliable place to see them. Even here it can be something of a lottery depending on weather and feeding conditions. Calm, sunny evenings are a good bet.

The first arrive in early April but numbers build up in June and July when lots of non-breeders visit the colony. Most depart by early August. Puffins do not breed until they are five years of age but they must visit the colony in their younger years to learn the social behaviours necessary to attract a mate and breed. They are monogamous; look carefully and you may see a courting pair bill rubbing – renewing their pair bond after a long winter apart out at sea.

Black Guillemot

Length: 35cm

←—————→

Breeding Status: Abundant

● ● ● ●

Habitat: Cliffs

A Tystie is the emblem of the Shetland Bird Club. Breeding adults are unmistakable with their oily black plumage and large white wing patch. Look carefully and you might see their striking red legs and mouth. They are well distributed around the coast breeding in loose colonies on boulder beaches, and in nooks and crannies in cliff faces.

Unlike our other auks which lay just one egg, the Tystie has a clutch of two. This may be a product of its more inshore lifestyle where it feeds on a wider variety of fish species than the other auks. Clutch size has evolved so as to deliver the maximum number of chicks over the lifetime of an adult. Long-lived species like seabirds may not breed at all in years when food is in short supply. Why risk the additional stresses of breeding which may result in death; it makes more sense to wait until next summer.

Razorbill

Length: 40cm

←——————→

Breeding Status: Abundant

● ● ● ●

Habitat: Cliffs

The Razorbill has blacker upperparts than the Guillemot, with clean white flanks a more pointed tail and a much deeper bill with white markings. Although pairs can often be seen perched on the cliffs, the egg is laid under boulders or in nooks in the cliff face. With effort, it is usually possible to find a Razorbill in a large seabird colony.

Their different bill shapes allow Guillemots, Puffins and Razorbills to all exploit energy rich sandeels. Guillemots carry one larger sandeel lengthways in the bill, Razorbills carry 4 or 5 moderate-sized sandeels across their bill and Puffins can carry as many as 20 or more small sandeels in their bill. Razorbills are typical of many seabirds, with both the male and female sharing incubating and chick-rearing duties.

Guillemot

Length: 42cm

Breeding Status: Abundant

● ● ● ●

Habitat: Cliffs

Guillemots nest in noisy, messy dense colonies. Their pointed bills, browner plumage and dusky markings along their flanks, separate them from the Razorbill. Look for bridled individuals – those that have a white line running around, and back from their eye. About 22% of Shetland birds show these 'spectacles'

Guillemot chicks fledge after just three weeks, barely a third the size of the adult and unable to fly. The male calls persistently to his chick, until finally it plucks up the courage to jump into the sea. The two swim off together, many to the Norwegian coast. The myth that a Guillemot's egg-shape has evolved so that when knocked it rolls in a circle rather than falling off the ledge has finally been exposed. It is more likely that this shape minimises the potential for harmful bacteria to enter the egg.

Common Tern

Length: 36cm

◄—————►

Breeding Status: Scarce

● ● ○ ○

Habitat: Low coastline

Although Common Terns generally arrive back in Shetland earlier than Arctic Terns, they are soon outnumbered by their more common cousin.

Separating Common and Arctic Terns can be challenging even for experienced birdwatchers. When perched, it is best to focus on the bill colour and pattern but in flight concentrate on the outer wing. Common Tern has a longer, distinctly more orange-toned red bill, typically with a fairly obvious blackish tip. Arctic Tern tends to show a shorter more blood red bill, sometimes with a black tip. The upperwing of an adult Common Tern typically shows a dirty dark wedge on the outer primaries (outer wing) whereas this area is typically a cleaner more uniform grey in Arctic. The Arctic Tern also tends to look more compact in flight with a longer tail.

Arctic Tern

Length: 36cm

←——————→

Breeding Status: Abundant

● ● ● ●

Habitat: Low coastline, islands in fresh water lochs and moorland

Arctic Terns probably see more sunlight than any other species on Earth, breeding at high northern latitudes and wintering deep in the southern hemisphere. Small recording devices fitted to some Arctic Terns have revealed that they fly over 50,000 miles during the course of a year – incredibly over their lifetime this is the equivalent of flying to the moon and back.

Arctic Terns are extremely aggressive parents and if the breeding season is progressing well, which is a rare event in recent years, they will repeatedly dive-bomb intruders into the colony. It is not unusual for them to draw blood so you are well advised to give breeding tern colonies a wide berth. The arrival of this species more than any other, defines the start of true spring in Shetland.

Kittiwake

Length: 39cm

Breeding Status: Abundant

● ● ● ●

Habitat: Cliffs

The Kittiwake is rarely seen away from the coast except when it is collecting mud for its nest. The only confusion species in Shetland is the Common Gull but the Kittiwake differs in having a solid black, dipped-in-ink wingtip and black legs. Its onomatopoeic call – 'kitt-e-wake' also helps identify it!

Sandeels form the staple diet of many of Shetland's seabirds but since the 1980s they have been in short supply in Shetland waters. This has led to a decline in several species and one of the hardest hit has been the Kittiwake. The population is now just 10% of what it was in 1981! Recent research has shown that some Shetland breeders head across the Atlantic to spend the winter off the coast of North America.

Black-headed Gull

Length: 37cm

←——→

Breeding Status: Common

● ● ● ○

Habitat: Islands in lochs and wetlands

This is the only gull likely to be seen in Shetland with a dark chocolate-brown hood. The combination of a white leading edge to the wing and a dusky area on the underside of the outer wing is distinctive in flight. Usually found in colonies although the location of some of these colonies can vary from year to year. The colony at the holm in Tingwall Loch is reliable.

Like many gulls and waders the Black-headed Gull is often found in flocks, sometimes mixed with other species. Flocking behaviour may occur for several reasons. It reduces the chances of a particular individual being predated, allows abundant food sources to be exploited and may well have a role in transferring information between individuals.

Common Gull

Length: 43cm

◄――――►

Breeding Status: Abundant

● ● ● ●

Habitat: Rough grassland and moorland

Gulls are a tricky group for beginners to identify and it is best to start with the adults. The Common Gull has a more gentle expression than the larger Herring Gull, and also differs in its smaller, wholly yellowish-green bill, dark eye and yellowish-green legs. The Kittiwake shares its dark eye and yellowish bill but has black legs and a wholly black wingtip that is not punctuated by white. The Kittiwake is also an almost exclusively coastal species.

The Common Gull is indeed the common inland gull in Shetland but this is not the case over much of Britain. Don't let its rather gentle expression fool you – it can be very aggressive in pursuit of food. They are quick to pinch a worm off nearby Lapwings or plovers, and can be seen chasing and killing newly fledged Starlings.

Lesser Black-backed Gull

Length: 52cm

◄─────────►

Breeding Status: Common

● ● ● ○

Habitat: Coasts and occasionally inland

The adult Lesser differs from the Great Black-backed Gull by its smaller size, thinner bill and longer wings, as well paler more slate grey upperparts, which contrast with the black wingtips, and yellow rather than pink, legs. They are the rarest of Shetland's large breeding gulls and generally breed on cliffs or rocky hillsides near the coast. A few may join mixed flocks of gulls when they gather inland, so it is worth checking any flocks that you come across.

This is the most aggressive of the large gulls in defence of its eggs and chicks, and particularly confident individuals will often strike the intruder – believe me, it can be painful!

Herring Gull

Length: 57cm

Breeding Status: Abundant

● ● ● ●

Habitat: Coasts, moorlands and towns

Adult Herring Gulls are best told from the closely related Lesser Black-backed Gull by their paler grey mantle and pink legs, and from the smaller Common Gull by their fiercer expression with their larger, yellow bill sporting a bright orange-red spot, and their pink not greenish-yellow legs.

In the past the Herring Gull was largely a coastal species in Shetland breeding on cliffs and feeding at sea, but in recent years the number of so-called 'urban' gulls has increased. These birds have responded to the increase in human waste – which usually offers them an easy meal – by moving into Lerwick and nesting on house roofs. They can be aggressive when protecting young and this doesn't always go down well with the householders!

Great Black-backed Gull

Length: 67cm

Breeding Status: Abundant

● ● ● ●

Habitat: Coasts and moorland

This is Shetland's largest breeding gull. It differs from the others in having very dark almost black upperparts that barely contrast with the black wingtips, pink legs and an impressively massive bill. They are more solitary nesters than their smaller cousins and favour coastal headlands, offshore stacks and moorland.

The species is well known as a fierce predator and this makes it unpopular with a lot of folk. It is not an uncommon sight to see an individual pursue Eider ducklings, and whole broods can be taken within just a few hours. They also frequently scavenge and can often be seen at road kills. Like most gulls, its jaws will unhinge to allow it to take larger prey whole.

Rock Dove

Length: 33cm

←—————→

Breeding Status: Common

● ● ● ○

Habitat: Caves along coasts coming to farmland and croft land to feed

The Rock Dove is the only dove in Shetland with pale grey plumage and a white rump and underwing. Although it breeds in caves along the cliffs it comes inland to feed and can form large flocks in weedy fields rich in seed, or on stubble with spilt grain. The Rock Dove is the ancestor of our 'town pigeons' and Shetland is one of few places in Britain where true native Rock Doves still exist.

The chicks are known as squabs and are fed on crop milk – a pale yellow substance with the consistency of cottage cheese, rich in protein and fat. This is produced in the adult's crop – a kind of pouch in the throat – a few days before the chicks hatch, and regurgitated to them until they are ready for solid food.

Wood Pigeon

Length: 40cm

<------->

Breeding Status: Scarce

● ● ○ ○

Habitat: Plantations and large gardens

Wood Pigeons are larger than Rock Doves with a yellow rather than dark bill, white neck patches and uniform grey wings lacking the two black bars shown by perched Rock Doves. In flight the Wood Pigeon has white wing patches and a grey rump and is distinctly heavier. In summer it is typically seen in, or close to, wooded areas and gardens.

Although the Wood Pigeon has been breeding in Shetland for 70 years, the population has only increased recently, probably as a result of the growth in plantations and creation of wooded gardens. It is still a challenging environment for them, however, and their nests which comprise little more than a small platform of twigs are frequently unable to withstand Shetland's windy climate.

Collared Dove

Length: 31cm

◄———————►

Breeding Status: Scarce

● ● ○ ○

Habitat: Gardens

Collared Doves are smaller, slimmer and longer-tailed than our other regularly occurring doves, with a distinctly beige-brown plumage. Look too for the narrow black half collar on the hind neck. Most Collared Doves occur in Shetland's more urban areas like Lerwick and Scalloway, as in winter they are dependent on garden feeders.

It is amazing to consider that the first British record of Collared Dove was not until 1955; this part of a spectacular range expansion from Asia that occurred in the 20th century. The first Shetland record was in 1960, and five years later they were breeding here. This is one of the first species to commence breeding in the islands with nest building starting as early as January in some years.

Merlin

Length: 30cm

←——————→

Breeding Status: Scarce

● ● ○ ○

Habitat: Moorlands

The Merlin is Britain's smallest falcon and the only bird of prey that breeds regularly in Shetland. The male is blue-grey above, the larger female is brownish. Both are most likely to be seen perching on a fence post, or dashing across moorland with their pointed but relatively short, angled, swept-back wings, and a medium length tail. They can be very persistent when chasing their prey. In Shetland, Meadow Pipits, Wheatears and Skylarks are the most common prey items.

Although both sexes will incubate the eggs the female tends do more than the male. Once the chicks have hatched they are usually brooded by the female, at least for the first week or ten days, with food being delivered to the female by the male.

Rook

Length: 45cm

Breeding Status: Common

● ● ● ○

Habitat: Kergord

Adults are easily told from Carrion Crows and Ravens by the greyish-white skin around the base of the bill. The individual in the photograph is an immature bird in which this feature has yet to fully develop.

Rooks nest colonially in rookeries, in which the dominant birds occupy the centre, leaving the less experienced individuals to breed at the edge. The only significant rookery in Shetland is at Kergord, although in recent years odd pairs have bred in Lerwick and Scalloway. Rooks have a poor reputation with some crofters yet their diet comprises mainly earthworms and insect larvae although they will eat cultivated grain.

Hooded Crow

Length: 47cm

Breeding Status: Common

● ● ● ○

Habitat: Cliffs, plantations, gardens and moorland

The grey and black plumage render it unmistakable. Until recently it was considered the same species as its all black southern counterpart, the Carrion Crow, which occurs in Shetland most years. The two interbreed and produce fertile offspring but the zone of hybridisation has remained narrow leading most taxonomic authorities to separate them into two species.

Crows are highly intelligent, skilled birds, quickly able to seize opportunities to exploit food sources. The Hooded Crow is the most heavily persecuted bird species in the islands as they are often implicated in the killing of lambs, or sheep in distress, and are also adept at taking the eggs and young of other bird species.

Hoodie Craa

Raven

Length: 60cm

←—————————→

Breeding Status: Common

● ● ● ○

Habitat: Cliffs, inland rock faces and plantations

The Raven is our largest corvid with a distinctly heavy, thick bill and often sports shaggy feathering on the throat. In flight it is long-winged with a distinctly diamond or wedge-shaped tail. The throaty 'prrrrk' call is also diagnostic.

Large flocks of non-breeders can often be seen during the summer months especially in the agriculturally rich South Mainland and around the landfill site north of Lerwick. These non-breeders have to wait until an opportunity arises to acquire a breeding territory, which are at a premium in Shetland. A large non-breeding population is often a sign that a species is faring well. This, despite the fact that Ravens are heavily persecuted in the islands, as although they are primarily a scavenger, they are quick to pounce on sheep that are in distress.

Goldcrest

Length: 9cm
◄►

Breeding Status: Rare
● ○ ○ ○

Habitat: Plantations and gardens

The Goldcrest is Britain's smallest bird and can weigh less than 5 grams! The combination of a plain looking face with its rather dark, staring eye and the golden-yellow crown with its dark borders is distinctive. Listen too for the very high-pitched contact call. Although migrants can turn up anywhere, it is generally restricted as a breeding bird to plantations and larger gardens with at least some conifers.

Like many small passerines Goldcrests have a relatively short life expectancy and therefore lay large clutches, typically numbering 9-12 eggs. Winter mortality can be high for small insect feeders – as much as 90%, and as few as 5% of birds from one generation actually contribute genes to the next generation.

Skylark

Length: 17cm

◄——►

Breeding Status: Abundant

● ● ● ●

Habitat: Grassland and moorland

Skylarks feed on the ground and during the summer are only likely to be confused with pipits whose streaked brown upperparts they share. The finely streaked buff breast, unmarked whitish belly, short crest and thick-based, pointed bill help to separate them on the ground. In flight Skylarks have a distinct white trailing edge to the wing and a more rippling call. The remarkable, often lengthy, hovering song flight can often be delivered from such great heights that it can be hard to see the bird.

Despite widespread declines in many parts of Britain, the species is faring well in Shetland where singing Skylarks are a constant feature of spring and summer. Exceptionally high breeding densities occur in Great Skua colonies and it is tempting to think that the skuas inadvertently offer them added protection from predators.

Swallow

Length: 19cm
←—→

Breeding Status: Scarce
● ● ○ ○

Habitat: Farm buildings, often feeding over fresh water or around cattle

Swallows spend much of their time on the wing, where the longish pointed wings, deeply forked tail, with long streamer-like outer tail feathers, and glossy blue-back upperparts and white underparts help to identify them. A few pairs breed in Shetland every year and some even manage to raise two broods. Youngsters from the first brood will sometimes help to raise chicks in the second brood.

The male's long tail streamers are a product of sexual selection; the longer his tail feathers are the more attractive he is to a female. Swallows are of course one of our long distance migrants, many travelling down as far as South Africa to spend the winter.

Chiffchaff

Length: 11cm
◄►

Breeding Status: Rare
● ○ ○ ○

Habitat: Plantations and gardens

Unless they are singing, separating a Chiffchaff from a
Willow Warbler can be taxing for even an experienced
birder. The songs are very different – the Chiffchaff's
a rather monotonous onomatopoeic 'chiff-chaff' the
Willow Warbler's a pleasant, if short, warble. Chiffchaffs
tend to have darkish horn-coloured legs and Willow's
paler orange-brown legs but this is not a hard and fast
rule. For the more technically minded, Willow Warbler
has a more striking head pattern, with a stronger
eyestripe and supercilium, and a less obvious eyering.
They are also longer-winged.

Chiffchaffs have only recently begun to breed in
Shetland doubtless as a result of the increase in cover
of trees and shrubs. Breeding males fiercely defend a
small breeding range but will feed over a larger area.

Willow Warbler

Length: 12cm
↔

Breeding Status: Rare
● ○ ○ ○

Habitat: Plantations and gardens

The Willow Warbler, like the Chiffchaff, is a common migrant to Shetland in both spring and autumn but has only started to breed in the islands in recent years. It is slightly larger, longer-winged, brighter and more boldly marked than that species but for further differences see under Chiffchaff.

All birds moult (replace) their feathers every year. Feathers are subject to wear and tear so need to be replaced regularly. In most birds this is a gradual process so that the bird can continue to fly, although wildfowl and some seabirds become flightless during this period. The Willow Warbler is exceptional, however, as it replaces all of its feathers twice a year.

Blackcap

Length: 14cm

←→

Breeding Status: Rare

● ○ ○ ○

Habitat: Plantations and gardens

A very plain greyish warbler; the males have a black cap and the females a brown cap. Blackcaps often skulk deep in cover when their musical warbling song is the only thing that betrays their presence. A few males stop to sing for brief periods in suitable habitat during their spring migration but Kergord is the only site where breeding has occurred on more than one occasion.

The Blackcap is one species whose migratory behaviour has changed in recent years. Many of those breeding in central Europe now move to Britain to spend the winter whereas previously they would have headed south to the Mediterranean and North Africa. This is probably due to a warming of the climate but may also be linked to the increased provision of garden food during winter.

Wren

Length: 10cm
◀▶

Breeding Status: Abundant
● ● ● ●

Habitat: Coasts, moorlands, plantations and gardens

The Wren's brownish plumage, pale supercilium, small size and habit of cocking its very short tail, make it an easy bird to identify. Shetland has two special subspecies of Wren – the Shetland Wren found throughout Mainland and the islands, and the Fair Isle Wren, restricted to Fair Isle. These have evolved to be larger and darker than their counterparts in Britain and Europe, and they also possess a flatter song.

In Shetland, many of our Wrens breed along the cliffs, using the geos as natural amphitheatres to project their song. The song is delivered very quickly – it lasts 7 seconds but comprises 100 different notes! Sheltered spots along the cliffs and seaweed-covered beaches probably hold more insect food then the more exposed hinterland. Hill burns and gardens are also favoured breeding haunts.

Starling

Length: 21cm

←———→

Breeding Status: Abundant

● ● ● ●

Habitat: Coasts and farmland

The Starling is a well-known, but somewhat under-appreciated species. Take a close look at a male pictured here (females have a more spotted appearance and a pink base to their bill) and see the strong lilac or greenish gloss to the plumage. They are also very clever mimics and can often fool observers into thinking that another species is singing. Some authorities consider Shetland Starlings to be a unique subspecies based largely on the dark plumage shown by juveniles in the islands.

Murmurations of Starlings are a popular sight on mainland Britain – flocks moving in unison with each individual mirroring the direction and speed of its nearest neighbour. On the UK mainland the population has declined markedly but here in Shetland, where agriculture is less intensive, the population is doing well.

Blackbird

Length: 26cm

◄————►

Breeding Status: Abundant

● ● ● ●

Habitat: Gardens

The all black male has an orange bill and eyering, is longer tailed than a Starling, hops much more and is usually solitary. The female is brown, with a paler throat and mottling on the breast and a duller bill. Breeding in Shetland was very rare in the 19th century but with the dramatic recent increase in planting garden trees and shrubs the population has grown markedly. A few pairs do, though, nest on the cliffs.

The Blackbird is one of the easiest birds to follow through the breeding season and it exhibits many typical songbird traits. They can breed when they are just one year old, the chicks hatch with their eyes closed and almost naked, both parents feed the chicks and remove faecal sacs from the nest, and both incubation and chick-rearing take about a fortnight each.

Robin

Length: 13cm
◄—►

Breeding Status: Rare
● ○ ○ ○

Habitat: Plantations and larger gardens

Robins first bred in Shetland in 1989, with just a handful of confirmed breeding records in the following 20 years. All of these breeding attempts were in the large, mixed, open plantations at Kergord. Several pairs breed there annually now and further pairs have also bred at other large gardens where there is a diverse mixture of trees, shrubs and flowers.

The Robin is a very common migrant to Shetland in early spring and late autumn and a few spend the winter in the islands. In spring, the male will bring his mate food to strengthen the pair bond but in winter it's a different story. Both males and females will defend their feeding territory aggressively.

Wheatear

Length: 16cm

←→

Breeding Status: Abundant

● ● ● ●

Habitat: Grasslands and moorland

The Wheatear is most readily identified by its white rump, and white tail with an inverted black T; the white is often apparent as the bird is flushed from the roadside. This is not a shy species. They are invariably out in the open, perching readily on rocks, walls, fences and fence posts, from which they boldy announce their presence with a harsh takking call. Fledged juveniles have spotted upperparts and underparts.

The Wheatear is probably the only songbird that breeds in North America and winters in sub-Saharan Africa. Some of these individuals may even pass through Shetland on migration. Astonishingly, minute tracking devices fitted to these birds have shown that some fly over 18,000 miles, before returning to their breeding grounds again!

House Sparrow

Length: 15cm
←—→

Breeding Status: Abundant
● ● ● ●

Habitat: Gardens and farmland

This species is familiar to everyone, and following introductions to many parts of the world and its ability to adapt to man, is probably the most widely distributed bird species on the planet. Although the demise in traditional crofting practices in Shetland since the 1970s has certainly seen a reduction in our House Sparrow population, this decline is far less dramatic than those experienced over much of Britain. Large flocks can still be seen in the South Mainland of Shetland where cereal crops are grown.

The House Sparrow is a very sociable bird, breeding in close proximity and engaging in communal dust and water bathing, and even communal singing. House Sparrows often mate for life which is unusual in a small songbird.

Grey Wagtail

Length: 19cm

Breeding Status: Rare

● ○ ○ ○

Habitat: Fast-flowing, rocky burns

In summer, adult males like the one pictured here, have black bibs bordered by a smart white moustachial stripe, and a white stripe above the eye. Their underparts are washed with a bright yellow, brightest under the tail. In females the throat is either dusky or white and the underparts are an altogether paler yellow. Grey Wagtails probably breed most years in Shetland but may be under-recorded.

The tail movements are particularly exaggerated in this species as it bobs and dashes along its favoured habitat – fast flowing rocky burns – chasing its insect prey. They may serve as a form of communication; telling other wagtails that this particular stretch of water is already occupied.

White Wagtail

Length: 18cm

Breeding Status: Scarce

● ● ○ ○ ○

Habitat: Coasts and burns

Two different subspecies occur in Shetland. The White Wagtail (as in the photo) has ash-grey upperparts, contrasting markedly with the black nape, crown, throat, chin and bib. The male Pied Wagtail has jet black upperparts rather than ash-grey, and these are replaced with a dark sooty-grey in the female. Both subspecies share the slim-line appearance and long black and white tail, which is almost constantly wagged up and down. In Shetland they typically nest in banks or roadside cuttings and are usually seen feeding on flat areas such as roadsides, car-parks, heavily grazed fields or lawns.

As soon as they return in the spring the male Pied Wagtail will set up and defend his territory. They can be very aggressive in defence of this territory, some will even attack reflections of themselves in window panes.

Meadow Pipit

Length: 15cm
◄—►

Breeding Status: Abundant
● ● ● ●

Habitat: Moorlands and grassland

Telling Shetland's two resident pipits apart can prove
tricky. Both are almost wholly terrestrial although
they will happily perch on fences and walls. Meadow
Pipits look altogether cleaner and more distinctively
marked than Rock Pipits. They have warmer, browner
upperparts with neat but distinct dark streaking, and
creamy white underparts with even more distinctly
marked dark streaking. They also have pale orangey-
brown legs as opposed to the dark legs shown by
Rock Pipits.

This is one of Shetland's most common songbirds.
It is not uncommon to flush a parent off of a nest as
they often breed in linear features like grassy roadside
verges or overgrown field boundaries. The nest cup is
beautifully woven and well hidden, typically containing
4 or 5 eggs. Look for the adults superb parachuting
song flight.

Rock Pipit

Length: 16cm
◄—►

Breeding Status: Abundant
● ● ● ●

Habitat: Coasts

The Rock Pipit is larger than the Meadow Pipit and also differs in having darker more olive-grey upperparts with diffuse streaking, and dirtier more sullied underparts, also with more diffuse streaking. The legs are typically dark and the outer tail feathers flash greyish-white, not clean white as in the Meadow Pipit.

The Rock Pipit is generally a more coastal species than the Meadow Pipit, especially in the breeding season. It particularly favours areas where seaweed has washed ashore and started to rot, providing an abundance of insect food. It is commonly encountered on coastal walks where it will often flit along the coast just in front of you calling nervously, a sign that the nest is close by.

Chaffinch

Length: 15cm
◄—►

Breeding Status: Rare
● ○ ○ ○

Habitat: Plantations

With his blue-grey crown and nape, rich pink face and underparts, white wing bars, reddish-brown back, green rump and white in the tail, the male Chaffinch is distinctive. The female shares the white wings bars and tail but is an altogether duller greyish-green above and off-white below.

Although there were occasional breeding records throughout the twentieth century the Chaffinch has never established a permanent breeding presence in the islands despite the increase in plantations and large gardens. Although seeds and other plant material comprise most of the diet in winter, breeding birds feed their chicks on invertebrates, especially caterpillars. Perhaps suitable prey is just in too short supply in Shetland. The Chaffinch is unusual for a songbird as it raises only one brood a year.

Linnet

Length: 13cm
←→

Breeding Status: Rare
● ○ ○ ○

Habitat: Farmland and gardens of South Mainland

The red forehead and breast, grey head and chestnut mantle are distinctive in the male. The female is much duller and could be confused with a Twite, although the grey bill and streaking on the throat will serve to tell them apart. Linnets first bred here in 1977 but since 2000 breeding has been annual and there are now quite a few pairs in the South Mainland.

The colonisation of Shetland is perhaps surprising given that the British population has shown a widespread decline due to the increase in use of herbicides and habitat loss. Most finches ensure that their chicks are fed at least some insects as protein is important for growth but Linnet chicks are fed almost exclusively on seed. The male regurgitates food to the female, who in turn, regurgitates it to the chicks.

Twite

Length: 13cm
◄—►

Breeding Status: Common
● ● ● ○

Habitat: Coasts and weedy areas

The Twite is often considered the northern counterpart of the Linnet. It differs from that species mainly by its unmarked buffy throat and pale yellowish bill, although the latter can appear darker in the breeding season. A male is pictured here; it shows a pink rump unlike the female. Listen for the onomatopoeic, nasal call, which is uttered frequently.

The Twite was much more common in Shetland in the past when traditional crofting practices were widespread. It was often considered a pest and local crofters killed many. In recent years the acreage of grain and root crops, which harbour many arable weeds that are important seed sources for Twite, has decreased further, placing even more pressure on this charming little finch.

Common Redpoll

Length: 12cm
◄─►

Breeding Status: Rare

● ○ ○ ○

Habitat: Plantations and larger gardens

A small finch easily identified when adult by the combination of a red patch on the forehead and the small area of black that extends above the bill, in front of the eye and on to the chin. Males can sometimes show a rich reddish flush on the breast too. When displaying, the males will undertake a noisy, bouncing song flight but once the eggs are laid the pair become very wary and are more often heard than seen. This is another species that seems to have colonised Shetland in the last few years, presumably as a result of the increase in the number of suitable plantations.

Redpolls can store food in an expandable part of their throat and digest it later, a handy way of exploiting a rich but short-lived food source. They are also very adept at hanging upside down when feeding.

Siskin

Length: 12cm
◄►

Breeding Status: Rare
● ○ ○ ○

Habitat: Plantations and gardens

The Siskin is a small, short-tailed finch with a longish, pointed conical bill. The plumage is quite distinctive being a combination of black, yellow, green and white. The black cap and chin is missing in the female. Another recent colonist, breeding is now annual in the large plantation at Kergord and around the gardens of Lerwick, both places where there are a good number of conifers.

Siskins are social birds outside the breeding season but will also breed in close proximity. One unusual feature of this species is that subordinate birds within a group will regurgitate food for more dominant members of the same sex. This may help reduce aggression in the flock.